I CAN'T BE AN ALCOHOLIC BECAUSE...

Hazelden
Always, the pioneer

"I Can't Be An Alcoholic Because..."
Fallacies and Misconceptions about Alcoholism

It is a common saying among alcoholics that the alcoholic is always the last person to know that he or she has a problem with drinking.

Spouse, family, employer, friends, and sometimes even the police know it long before the alcoholic will admit that drinking is causing trouble. And as long as the alcoholic refuses to accept the fact that drinking is causing trouble he will do nothing about the problem.

There are many misconceptions about the nature of alcoholism in our midst which keep the alcoholic from seeing, recognizing or admitting a drinking problem.

Here are some of the common ones.

I can't be an alcoholic because...
- I am not a skid row bum
- I never drink before 5:00 p.m.
- I never drink anything but beer
- I drink only on weekends
- I can quit anytime

I Can't Be An Alcoholic Because I Am Not A Skid Row Bum

This is the most common fallacy among alcoholics and the general public. The idea that the only person who could possibly be alcoholic is the "falling-down drunk" on skid row is, unfortunately, a misconception.

But most people do not know that the skid row denizen represents only about three percent of our nation's 10,000,000 alcoholics. The other 97% are ordinary people, most of whom still have good jobs, are maintaining their families, and are "getting along," although often having a difficult time because of their drinking.

Any person can be or become an alcoholic. I personally have known priests, ministers, lawyers, doctors, teachers, salesmen, businessmen, carpenters, housewives, and stenographers who were alcoholics. But not one of them was on skid row.

Alcoholism can affect anyone. So don't let the fact that you still have a job, are making good money, and still living at home fool you into thinking that you don't need to do anything about your drinking if you frequently drink to intoxication, or if you have trouble stopping when others do.

If you have lost the ability to say "NO" to a drink or to control the **amount** you drink, you have a drinking problem, and don't kid yourself!

People in all walks of life are alcoholics because they have become dependent upon harmful quantities of alcohol. They have developed a physiological addiction coupled with a psychological compulsion which destroys their ability to control their drinking or to behave responsibly when drinking.

If a person so addicted continues to drink, he or she will eventually, in all probability, become unemployable even though it may take a good number of years to reach that stage.

We must never forget that alcoholism, or addiction to alcohol, is a progressive and fatal disease. The only hope, the only way the alcoholic can save his or her life, is to learn to live without alcohol.

Because I Never Drink Before 5:00 p.m.

Some people have the mistaken idea that they are not alcoholics until they have to have a drink in the morning. This is not true.

It is not **when** one drinks, but whether one can control the amount of drinks that determines whether there is a drinking problem.

By "loss of control" I do not mean that a person gets drunk every time he or she drinks, but that he or she very often drinks more than intended, and drunkeness occurs with increasing frequency. Anyone who "just has to have" a drink no matter when — at lunch, after work, before dinner, at bedtime — is in danger of becoming dependent upon alcohol. From dependence upon alcohol it is not far to addiction. Dr. William B. Terhune, psychiatrist with The Neurological Institute in New York says, **"Never** take a drink when you 'need' one."

It is true that the need for a "morning drink" is one of the symptoms of the crucial or chronic stages of alcoholism. But simply because one does not crave a drink in the morning does not rule out the disease of alcoholism.

Again, it is the loss of control that determines whether a person is an alcoholic, or whether alcohol is causing continuing trouble in some area of one's life. In fact, if your spouse is insisting that your drinking is excessive, that is one of the best signs that it really is a problem, and you ought to do something about it! Your trouble is never going to get better as long as you drink. It will only get worse.

Because I Never Drink Anything But Beer

Many people mistakenly believe that beer has a low alcohol content and is less intoxicating or addicting than gin, whiskey, vodka, or wine. However, it is the chemical ethyl alcohol, C_2H_5OH, to which the alcoholic is "allergic," and this chemical is found in all alcoholic beverages. There is about as much ethyl alcohol in an average can of beer as there is in a 4-ounce glass of wine or a one-ounce shot of whiskey.

To determine the amount of "absolute alcohol" in any drink, simply multiply the number of ounces in the drink by its percentage of alcohol. For example, a twelve-ounce serving of 4.5% beer contains a .54 ounce of absolute alcohol. A one-ounce shot of 100-proof whiskey (which is about 50% alcohol) contains half an ounce of absolute alcohol. An ordinary four-ounce serving of wine (with a 15 or 20% alcoholic content) contains .60 or .80 ounce of absolute alcohol.

It is the chemical ethyl alcohol which is the intoxicating and addicting ingredient in every alcoholic beverage. This alcohol is burned up in the body by the liver at a fixed rate. If alcohol is consumed in whatever vehicle — whiskey, beer, gin, vodka, or whatnot — at a rate faster than the liver can metabolize it, intoxication is bound to result. Some of my friends (who insist they are not alcoholics because they drink only beer) tell me, however, that they often drink from 10 to 15 or more cans of beer in an evening. This is the equivalent of 10 to 15 or more shots of whiskey.

Because I Drink Only On Weekends

Many people believe that the only person who is an alcoholic is one who drinks great quantities everyday, or is drunk all the time. But many alcoholics can go a long time without taking a single drink.

Some alcoholics can stay dry for weeks, months, or even years. So it is not when or how often one drinks that determines a drinking problem. Rather it is the inability to control one's actions, or the amount consumed while drinking.

A woman may drink only on weekends, but if she often or regularly gets drunk on weekends, she certainly has a drinking problem. If a man's drinking causes him continuing difficulty in any area of his life — job, family, health — or is costing him more than he should be spending, he needs help.

And what about your weekend drinking? Is that the high point of your week? Do you look forward to it with great anticipation and find it hard to wait until Friday night? Would your weekend be spoiled if you couldn't drink?

In some cases, the **meaning** of one's drinking is more significant than the amount. Remember Hancock's Law: **"The more important your drug of choice is to you, the more it means to you, the more you feel that it does for you, the more trouble you are going to have with it."**

Every person who drinks should take a very careful look at his or her drinking. The little grandmother who has a glass of wine on Christmas Eve, and that's it for the year, is not going to have much of a problem with alcohol. But the person who feels a need to drink in order to be accepted or to project a certain image; one who drinks to deal with boredom, frustration, loneliness, anxiety; who drinks to cope or change the way he or she feels; or one who cannot have a good time or be comfortable without alcohol — that drinker is headed for trouble sooner or later.

Because I Am Too Young

Another common fallacy about problem drinking is that a person must be at least fifty or sixty years old to become an alcoholic. It is not your age nor how many years you've been drinking, but what drinking is doing to you and whether you have control over it, that determines whether alcohol is a problem. Whenever a person becomes dependent upon alcohol and has lost control of his or her drinking, or has repeated trouble related to it, then that person has a serious problem and must do something about it now!

Loss of control can occur at any time in a person's drinking career. In treatment centers we are seeing more and more young people, often in their early teens, who become intoxicated every time they drink, even though they do not want or intend to. I remember such a young woman who celebrated her sixteenth birthday while in our treatment center. She was truly an alcoholic.

Age has very little to do with alcoholism. It can attack a person at almost any age. The young man or woman who repeatedly gets drunk intentionally or unintentionally is already in trouble and may be "hooked."

Because I Can Quit Any Time

When did you last "go on the wagon" and why? It was undoubtedly because your drinking was giving you some trouble.

Drinkers who are not alcoholic do not need to go on the wagon, for they are always able to control their drinking. Alcoholics go on the wagon to try to prove to themselves and others that they can still control their drinking, or that they can go without it. Inevitably they discover they can't do it. When persons have lost control over their drinking, there is no compromise with total abstinence; they will never be able to drink safely again. This truth has been proven by the painful personal "research" of a million members of A.A. over the past 45 years.

It doesn't really matter how many days you can go without a drink. Most alcoholics can manage for one reason or another to live for fairly long periods without alcohol. Far more significant and important is this: How do you feel during those periods of forced abstinence? Are you happy, calm, relaxed, even-tempered? Or are you nervous, tense, easily frustrated, irritable, resentful, anxious, lonely, depressed? If such is the case, then you are simply experiencing what A.A. members call a "dry drunk," and with this kind of mental attitude you will sooner or later resume drinking. And it will inevitably cause you trouble again.

The reason for this is that, for you, alcohol has become a drug or a "medicine" rather than just a beverage. You are drinking for a specific result — to change the way you feel, rather than merely to enjoy a social occasion. You have to drink again to deal with your uncomfortable feelings: boredom, anger, insomnia, depression, loneliness. In the alcoholic, these mental states are often symptoms of the illness. A depression which precedes or follows a loss of control in drinking is a serious and much-to-be-heeded warning sign. And if your emotional miseries are relieved by your return to drinking, it could mean that you are already "hooked" — dependent upon alcohol to help you manage your life.

The point, then, is not whether you can **stop** anytime, but whether you have to **start** again and whether the drinking resumes at a harmful level with loss of control. Compulsive behavior with regard to the use of a chemical indicates the presence of addiction. Any unplanned or unpredictable behavior connected with the uncontrolled use of alcohol is a certain indication that you have a serious drinking problem, and a problem that is certain to get worse if you continue to drink.

Finally, ask yourself honestly whether your drinking, even in spite of periods of enforced abstinence, has become worse, or whether it is now causing you more trouble than it was, say, two to five years ago. Has there been any disintegration of your relationships within the family, with your friends, employers, or fellow workers due to your problem drinking? Has your drinking caused trouble between you and your spouse, parents, children, or friends? If so, consider the possibility that the fault may not be entirely theirs. It may be that you are sick, the **unknowing** victim of the disease of alcoholism.

The late Dr. E.M. Jellinek, who is recognized as one of the world's greatest pioneer authorities on alcoholism, pointed out that continued excessive drinking seriously affects one's powers of reason, impairs judgment, and destroys the ability to look at one's self critically or to evaluate accurately one's own actions and attitudes — especially the depth of personal involvement with alcohol. This explains why the alcoholic can honestly believe "I can quit anytime," when the truth is exactly opposite.

FORGET THE WORD "ALCOHOLIC"!

Yes! I beg you, throw that word out the window and never use it again. No one wants to be labeled and put into that box even though most people think they know what "alcoholic" is. So don't get hung up or defensive about whether you are or are not a so-called alcoholic. It really doesn't matter whether you are an alcoholic or a purple-eyed creature from Mars.

The important questions are: What is drinking doing to your life, to your relationships, to your work, to your sense of responsibility, to your value system, and to your peace of mind? What kinds of problems are consistently related to your drinking? Would your family be happier if you were to quit drinking entirely?

You don't have to be an "alcoholic" to have problems with alcohol. Anyone who drinks can have some kind of trouble with it, sometimes. If your only problem with drink is that your spouse is objecting to it, then you must decide whether drinking is more important than your marriage. And if it is, then without question you do have a drinking problem, and you'd better do something about it. Compulsive drinking, if it continues untreated, becomes a fatal disease.

Actually, alcoholism is nothing more than a type of drug dependence. Yes, alcohol is a DRUG! which can harmfully affect one's health, emotional life, social relationships, and responsibilities. One definition says that people have alcoholism when they continue to drink in spite of their own best interests, and in spite of painful and harmful consequences. However, impaired thinking often prevents the problem drinker from seeing the connection between the drinking and the problems.

IGNORANCE CAN KILL YOU

And so can stubbornness, or the refusal to face the facts. But honest acceptance of the truth can free you from the chains of addiction to alcohol, and thus save your life. Don't be misled by the old common fallacies about drinking and alcoholism. And don't be fooled into thinking, "I can't be an alcoholic because I'm not a skid row bum, I never drink before 5:00 o'clock, I never drink anything but beer, I drink only on weekends, I am too young, or I can quit any time."

Unfortunately, part of the nature of alcoholism is its tendency to deceive and delude its victims so that they cannot recognize they are sick. They can no longer look at themselves and their behavior objectively. Alcohol has diminished their capacity for accurate self-evaluation and self-judgment. It's like trying to shave in a foggy mirror. They honestly believe "I can quit anytime," but do not understand or realize that when it comes to drinking they are no longer in control.

If there are any harmful consequences related to your drinking, if you are getting into any kind of trouble with it, get help before your problems get worse. For you can be certain that if you continue to drink, they **will** get worse. Alcoholism is a progressive, fatal disease if not treated.

If you want to drink, that's your business. If you need to stop, there is help available. If you want help, or if you have a relative or friend who needs help, go to the phone book and call Alcoholics Anonymous, an alcoholism information or treatment center, or use the toll-free number on the back of this pamphlet to call Hazelden.

Hazelden
Always, the pioneer

Another book that will interest you...

Thirst for Freedom
by David A. Stewart

Sobriety can be a thrilling adventure, a positive, creative experience rather than just a state of abstinence.

Freedom from addiction is much more than simply recovery from a former state of poor health. It means living a productive, happy, and abundant life through personal and spiritual growth.

The author surveys the entire field of addictions and develops the concept of empathy — the art of putting yourself in the other person's place — as the chief technique in achieving creative sobriety.

Order No. 1080   366 pages

For price and order information, please call one of our Customer Service Representatives.

Hazelden
Educational Materials

Box 176, Center City, MN 55012
(800) 328-9000 (Toll Free. Cont. U.S. Only.)
(800) 328-0500 (Toll Free. Film and Video Orders. Cont. U.S. Only.)
464-8844 (Toll Free. Metro Twin Cities.)
(612) 257-4010 (MN & Outside Cont. U.S.)

Order No. 1340   ISBN: 0-89486-158-1